WHERE WE GREW UP

Jennifer Lagier

FUTURECYCLE PRESS

www.futurecycle.org

Published by FutureCycle Press
Lexington, Kentucky, USA

ISBN 978-1-938853-92-0

for Nona and fellow rural refugees

CONTENTS

WHERE WE GREW UP

The walls had hooks,
wire barbs reaching from stucco
to rip a child's skin.
From time to time,
fireballs would spin
around the asphalt kitchen floor;
drain pipes gave off an odd glow
beneath the yellow-tiled sink.

I remember the hot breath
of some invisible presence
standing between my sister and me,
alone and afraid
in our maple twin beds.
Dad whimpered in his sleep;
mother turned and turned,
grinding her teeth.

Sometimes on hot summer evenings
we could hear the distant cries
of injured late-shift cannery workers
as they tried pulling crushed limbs
from relentless moving cogs
or assembly line belts.

The rising delta wind brought
their moaning pleas into stifling rooms
where we wept our way through bad dreams,
windows open as wide as they would go.
Every sound carried.

Fifties Flashback

A Sears repairman removed
the pegboard back of our giant
black and white TV, fussed inside.

He's cleaning out the dead cowboys,
Daddy told my sister and me
as we watched, open-mouthed.

I imagined cold, stiff piles
of shot-down desperadoes,
swept away with gray dust.

Now my father is gone; nights bring
blurry reruns of past peach harvests,
truck rides he gave us to the cannery and back.

At the grading station, he
hitched up perpetually sagging Levis,
handed me a quarter to purchase strawberry pop.

I miss our Saturdays, simple monochrome westerns,
Cisco and Pancho galloping to the rescue,
happy endings that last.

WITCH HUNT

You recall the tarnished rosaries
chanted weekly
to ward off bad blood,
remember the red pattern
tattooed by wire coat hangers
on a child's skin.

Frozen gray photos
from the Siberia of our attic
show the manicured party facade:
matching dresses, tiny hats,
patent leather shoes,
Sunday veils and white gloves.

You search for evidence among
nostalgia's boxed ruins,
find only the toxic soundtrack
which plays on endlessly, dropping
words like *incompetent, failure*
into dark seams.

Nightmares, fanged predators,
label every possible flaw.
You swallow whatever potion
will unwind the poisoned necklace of thorns,
undo a witch's curse,
remove the lethal apple pushed with love
down a little girl's throat.

CONFIRMATION

Ironically, it's a nun who
orders mother to purchase
my first pair of high heels,
nylons, the superfluous bra,
rubber straight-jacket girdle.
She tells me the vulnerable priest
needs these reminders to adorn
my pudgy, twelve-year-old body
so he won't succumb
to overwhelming desire.

I stare at Sister's drab habit,
imagine life beneath black cloth,
visualize her spartan cell,
untouched breasts, utilitarian panties.
I sit, listen in confusion,
ponder threats of hell
and her Catholic warnings.

Mother gleefully chooses
my size 15 tent dress:
two tones of heifer plaid
with immense rhinestone buttons.
I redden, sweat toward adulthood
within tight elastic.

When my turn comes to be confirmed,
I stumble forward on command
down the church aisle
dividing our class
into isolate genders.
Trembling and filled
with a devout sense of faith,
I kneel before a man wearing skirts,
feel him slapping my face.

Ditch Swimming

Every summer, an icy rush of melted snow pack
raced toward wilting orchards. Seduced by rumors
of heat relief, we biked dirt roads to back fields,
took the forbidden cold plunge.

Barefoot delinquents in wet shirts, torn cut-offs,
we defied parental warnings and prohibitions,
gleefully cannon-balled into subterranean grottoes
where jagged steel, hidden concrete blocks lurked.

Fat bullfrog tadpoles wriggled up
from tarry mud like mutated sperm.
Rotting peaches rotated in slow circles
around green algae, creamy pesticide foam.

1958 Fruit Cutting Shed

In that sweltering tin shed
upon sandy floors,
I learn about cruising, French
kisses, and the Ronettes.

I am nine years old,
a new knife
and sack lunch of salami
clamped in sweaty hands.

My pay: a quarter
per enormous lug box.
I cut peaches
from daybreak to dusk.

Children stand on pallets,
slice sticky fruit,
sing with the radio
as the sulfur fumes sting.

My future husband,
the ten-year-old shed boy,
removes layers of peach halves
when I shout "Trays away!"

June, July, August...
I earn less than ten dollars.
My fingers harden,
bleed.

SMALL GAME COLLECTOR

I was the hunter,
tracker of totems,
stalked jackrabbits
through Johnson grass thickets.

Along ditch banks, I turned
cement chunks, seized
gliding commas of garter snakes,
blue-bellied lizards.

My fingers snatched
nervous swallowtails
from carnival clumps
of blooming lantana.

I enclosed each savage pulse
in the net of my acquisitive hand,
patrolled childhood's frontiers
to drag home the untamed.

SUMMER OF LOVE

It's a warm Central Valley night.
You are a 16-year-old Italian Catholic virgin,
half undressed and uncomfortably wedged
between the bucket seats
of your steady boyfriend's blue Mustang.
After months of his begging, you finally give in.
As he tears his way into you,
a drunk careens from the river bank willows,
peers through the windshield,
passes out on the car hood.

So this is passion,
the romantic act of becoming *one*
you tell yourself
despite embarrassment, pain.
Outside, the homeless bum twitches.
You wonder what happens now.
All the way home, you feel you've been cheated.

TIME DEPOSIT

Back then,
salesmen ate DDT
by the handful
to demonstrate it was safe.

Children rode sawhorses around
burning parathion-sack bonfires,
drank from stained hose ends
dangled into tanks
of pesticide spray rigs.

Dioxin decorated
ripped valley earth
like powdered sugar.

In metallic blue orchards,
kids dodged rainbow plane drift
to wave at crop duster pilots.

Wandering past unread warning signs,
we chewed clingstone peaches
unwashed from the fields.

Now we carpool to chemotherapy,
yearly family funerals,
draw down poison's interest:
postponed carcinoma.

Toxic House

"In this house where no one survives love..."
—*Ruth Daigon*

Through a streaked window, I saw Dad crying in the orchard
after losing one more fight with my razor-tongued mom.

Daily, asbestos seeped from floor tiles. Our walls spit green fire,
witnessed a thousand small deaths.

Corroded pipes carried cold water and diluted dioxin
from underground well to drinking glass.

Mother shrieked at our incompetence as workers.
Resentment passed from knotted heart to child-striking hands.

This is the place we broke, grew twisted, learned
how to cover the bruises, never verbalize pain.

RIPE FOR THE PICKING

Dioxin-laced showers
blown from machines
whisper immortality,
cling to bare skin,
dormant peaches and grapes.

Jackrabbits
and valley quail
wipe feathers
and fur upon saturated grass,
track home lethal dew.

In spring,
sprayed limbs blossom,
set a bumper crop
of poisonous apricots,
cherries and apples.

By September we harvest
tons of Trojan-horse fruit,
celebrate and feast
upon what we have nurtured.

Inside us, secret germinations
extend lethal roots
for dark seasons to come.

Family Dinners

"God is thinking about me and eating me..."
—*Tomaž Šalamun*

During Sunday mass,
we fidgeted on hard pews,
light-headed from overnight fasting,
suffused with delusions
of impending salvation.

We bargained with God,
admitted our failures.
With bent heads, we knelt,
offered trembling tongues
for dry wafer flesh
from the sacrificed Christ.

Family dinners reinforced
the repentance theme:
fried onions and leathery liver,
a hungry child's crown of thorns.

Mother's "eat three bites
or sit all night" rule
taught me to swallow
in obedient silence
everything I was told,
growing glutted, then sick,
from the burden of Catholic grace.

Later, I tortured myself
for becoming a victim.
Stuck a finger down my throat
and rejected it all,
reclaiming control
as I obstinately purged.

SMALL TOWN SEX EDUCATION

It was the summer
high school boys bloomed
with octopus hands,
inescapable tongues,
atomic erections.

We compared contraceptive folklore
at slumber parties,
girls with awakening hormones
in shortie pajamas.
I learned how to smoke
filterless Pall Malls,
rat my hair,
kill militant semen.

Virginity seized me
in one vengeful claw,
whispered horror stories
of unwanted pregnancy
into my ear
using nun's voices.

I got tired of wrestling fingers
out of my panties, went on a
private hunger strike
against sexual freedom.
Punished appetite with hours of leg lifts,
solo runs around my dad's orchard.

Pinned baggy skirts as they fell
from my waist to the
tails of my empty-tent blouses.
Watched myself shrink
back to the safety
of flat-chested childhood.

AUGUST IN ESCALON

Here in the land of
churches and gas stations,
we move sparingly and slow
in the simmering heat.

Peach fuzz rises with the sun.
Days, over-exposed and glittering,
melt into the same twenty-four hours
of recycled white noise.
Asphalt softens like canal bank mud
around concrete malls.

Outside, roses cremate
themselves colorless;
blackbirds haven't the energy
to flap or complain.

A slow freight screams,
drags itself toward the cool Pacific,
steel and grease churning
along burning rails.

I sweat, lean into the open vents
of a straining swamp cooler—
nineteen, pregnant, newly married—
wonder how the hell
we ever made it this far.

ACCEPTING THE HABIT

Penguins
we called those
Brides of Christ
who knelt
to escape burning dreams
in their celibate beds.

After Catechism
we practiced mortal sin
with boys tutored by dirty magazines,
pretended the hands
inside our bras
belonged to actual men.

One by one
we tired of dreams
that refused to breathe,
took the easy out
and succumbed
to our grandmothers' myths.

After white weddings blessed
by priests, familiarity exorcised
the devil we originally craved,
left us in sexual poverty,
cloistered and chaste.

Now we confess to therapists,
perform treadmill penance;
Zoloft has become
our sacred communion of choice.

Last Supper

While other women
tore lettuce and arranged china,
I was in our hosts' bedroom,
undressing with your older brother.

Outside the closed door,
you speared smoked oysters,
jangled ice cubes, smoked,
drank your third V.O. and water.

The lasagna I brought
got too hot, burnt cheese
and singed tomato sauce
pouring smoke from the oven.

After, I paced
alone in the garden,
knew in a year I'd be gone,
this catastrophe over.

For the last time, we sat
together at the family table.
Your father lifted his wine glass;
you nervously touched me.

I looked into your Lazarus eyes,
delivered the final defiant kiss,
resurrected myself
with an act of betrayal.

Sleeping With the Cat

Hunger worms its way
beneath my skin
to unscratchable depths.

From night's lonely corners,
ghosts of men I have loved
come to circle my bed.

Unwanted and alone,
I cling to chilly pillows,
put my hands on myself.

Outside, a swollen moon hangs
above turgid squash,
miles of gaping gold blooms.

HOMETOWN REUNION

"Land of Peaches and Cream"
the familiar billboard
next door to a taxidermist's shop reads.

A failing fruit stand
displays softening mounds
of hollow-cored melons.

Here churches outnumber
gas pumps and grocery stores
by a two-to-one margin.

Driving by Bender's Bakery,
I still taste those
tough-skinned ice cream cones.

Cruising the concrete shores
of a fading Bud's Frosty, I discover
a balding high school alumnus.

He clutches a beer can,
just like the '60s,
irremovably rooted.

Puppet strings from our canal bank past
wave my jerking hand
in embarrassed remembrance.

I roll past the city limits of guilt,
return to my great expectations'
tragic innocence.

Death Watch

for the latest cancer cluster fatality

For months we have
charted shrinking intervals
between hospitalizations,
practiced grief in bearable increments.

Now we calendar a day or two at a time,
plan flexible weekends,
book only refundable rooms and
flights with no penalties
for quick cancellation.

Updates come morning and night
from the exhausted family members
who trade shifts and wait
in your hospital room.

Those at home have wept themselves dry,
rehearsed for the final
phone call they fear
but have grown to expect.

In our community,
we no longer bother
to guess which pesticide
triggered this cancer.

One by one, loved ones
sicken and suffer,
pray for deliverance,
slip through our fingers.

At the cemetery
we calculate our own
life expectancies, toxic exposures,
stand in diminishing circles.

HARD FROST

for my father, January 2009

A blasted world sparkles; cold sun glares
the morning my aunt calls to say he is gone.

Around me, poinsettias blacken and droop.
Our birdbath crackles with splinters of ice.

A widowed dove, lone survivor of hawk attack,
picks among fallen seeds.

THE HAUNTING

It comes in waves:
sadness, remembrance of loss,
constant fatigue.

I drag myself between gray hours,
required obligations,
see your closed eyes again.

Mourners touch your chilled skin,
visit loudly with one another
as if it's a party, not a final viewing.

You asked to have your ashes
scattered in a field by the spray rig.
We filed you in a mausoleum instead.

Every day since, I wander empty trails,
the last of our bloodline,
wonder when scar tissue forms.

GHOSTS

Last year, I drove you through orchard rows so we could
assess snowy blossoms, watch the rented bees swarm.

Square hives spilled a buzzing frenzy.
Almonds exploded into white popcorn blooms.

Today, ragged clouds swell above bruised horizons.
Ghostly tumbleweeds fly across sodden roads.

Your new John Deere tractor sits
wet and abandoned.

Cold winds rise and make me shiver.
Your assaulted trees moan.

Presence

You visit us nightly, drop in
to explain gardening secrets,
how to drape tender plants,
protect them from frost.

When my sister and I compare notes,
we discover you look in your forties,
muscular with callused hands,
walking again.

You come, wearing tan farmer's pants,
a faded work shirt, and ratty boots,
stomp across ancient levees
into our dreams.

Each morning, she and I
power walk beside ocean, debate
whether you try to warn or reassure.
Your constant presence brings peace.

Shame

Your mother says
she's the only woman
in her community
with two daughters
and six sons-in-law.

You are an embarrassment
with your temporary addresses,
suspicious political inclinations,
odd dietary habits,
come-and-go lovers.

She's ashamed
you failed as a farmwife,
couldn't keep
a good secretarial job
for over 30 years like her.

You are condemned to
live alone, never have children,
waste your life
surrounded by grubby artists
and slackers.

Every night she phones to criticize,
recite your offenses,
leave you with an earful of admonitions,
obligations, and a migraine
or worse.

Coffee Klatch

Something compels me
to visit the donut & coffee shop
where my dead father
and his cronies
used to hang out.
Farmers, ag supply salesmen
occupy every table, drink in
right-wing political commentary,
local gossip, sexist remarks—
not another woman in sight.
To even the odds,
I invite a female cousin
and my sister to join me
for a cup of terrible brew.
We commandeer our own space,
force men to move from chairs
they've called theirs over 35 years.
We shriek, compare men's laughter
to the sound of untuned Harleys,
share priceless phrases
we've just overheard.
Unable to adjust
to women with opinions,
geezers grumble;
we've invaded,
good-old-boy territory.
Twenty minutes later,
we've run off the last of them.
We declare the place ours,
a testosterone-free zone,
plan our next offensive,
tip the counter girl well.

IF THE SHOE FITS

These hands are direct descendants
of my Italian Great Nona
who excelled in impatience,
forever cutting and burning herself.

I inherited my mother's teeth,
sharp and strong from grinding
all night on unpalatable words
left politely unsaid.

This heart wears its
Catholic crown of thorns,
the scarred ruins of
too many wrong men.

From my father comes
the gift of laughter,
a need to make the earth bloom,
extra-wide farmer's feet.

ACKNOWLEDGMENTS

These poems, some in other versions, first appeared in the following publications:

"Hometown Reunion," *Lactuca,* No. 15, 1992
"1958 Fruit Cutting Shed," *Boomer Girls,* University of Iowa Press, 1999
"Small Town Sex Education," *Slipstream,* Issue No. 20 (2000)
"Accepting the Habit," *Italian Americana,* Vol. 18, No. 2 (Summer 2000)
"Sleeping With the Cat," *Kentucky Review,* 2015
"Shame," "Fifties Flashback," "Confirmation," "August in Escalon,"
    Syndic Literary Journal, No. 12, February 2015
"Where We Grew Up," "Witch Hunt," "Coffee Klatch," *Dead Snakes,*
    February 10, 2015

Cover artwork, treatments of a 1950s family photo by the author's mother, June Lewis, by Diane Kistner; back-cover photo by Laura Bayless; cover and interior book design by Diane Kistner; Charter text with Mate SC titling

www.ingramcontent.com/pod-product-compliance
Lightning Source LLC
Chambersburg PA
CBHW060046050426
42448CB00012B/3134